PLEASE PRESS

Sad Press
Bristol 2022

ISBN 978-1-912802-44-9
sadpresspoetry.com

PLEASE PRESS

Kat Sinclair

for est. fires
for gotten
for swore
for gone

It is a shame

The gulls are smaller here
still I beg the children on an old route to
lay me out on the silt
I want to be pecked at the liver so at least it would
mean something to someone
in the grand history of things
instead I am: like no one specific character or
touchstone
instead I am: grieving
in a time of a great and differing grief
no great Antigonist, no canonical specifics,
just that

I will someday issue an apology to everyone I know
for how much I have hated them
for not being me
yes, you too
you 'completely somebody else entirely not me' prick

Spots appearing on my face like my sixth
kindly Welsh woman
of the day I am a bundle of gratitude but they are
representative of if not actually
incapable of communicating
like I wish they would collaborate
just be one big spot I can drain
in one go and bathe in the consequences—
I am sorry, her Welshness is irrelevant
as is her kindliness, I am forgetting
my political economy, distracted by keypads
Like, I would steal your shopping lists
from your bins and find them
publishable
but more so actually I want to know
how you manage it:
cooking, colour,
I am certain you write well too

That'll do nicely
that'll be more than enough for the time being
just those, limpid pools
like that's something to be proud of

Please take the Oramorph away
I love your shoes
let's get lunch ten years ago
we would have been friends
you would have loved him
you might have noticed
I am slumped against the bannister again,
lamenting, pecking.

11/05/20

What if I wanted you to take me seriously for once like
when I say I wish there was a spoon handy
to crack the top of me,
peer in for the writhing electric mass of
that struggle, infinite capacity; finite grey meal
it drives me mad until I think I have reached
my capacity for madness
then I go a little madder, and I understand.

It's like I've always said: if you can't deplatform them,
ruin their marriage,
then burn the back of your neck like an effigy
sitting in the sun and thinking
with your hands sunk into an orange
wishing it were the palm of a friend's hand
or the storming of the Treasury Building
there are only two verbs left: to grip, and to plunge.

Please Press

I wander into the top floor of the government agency
to which I should not be able to gain access but it is a cupboard and nobody cares
anyway everyone is working from home today
so I sit on the floor of the cupboard and scream
HE! IS! DEAD! STOP TELLING HIM HE HAS TO FILE HIS TAX RETURNS!
and the sky opens up and the clouds tell me to please press one
please press one
please press
please
harder
until it splinters like a fake phone or carapace
into something like forgiveness or a letter opener
spikier than the last

I tell the puppy he is very special
then I feel real guilt for not having told my cuddly toys the same
when I did, once — and cried when they were taken away
because I had asthma and their stuffing rubbed me the wrong way

When the government agency was new I took great pride in knowing
that it was in fact a private enterprise in France
and would point to the signage and coo, disappointed,
like 'there it is and isn't it awful and aren't you glad I told you'
taking screenshots of the makeup of each department
like a cruel anatomist
these buildings they are still alive
only divvied up like pig parts and then again by me
in my interminable analysis
going nowhere but the hospital once again and pointing at the signs

Run in partnership with
all of us everywhere
with mirror image batons and pepper spray
what was once smallprint now
never even there

Was it written in ink?
Did we even check?

Help me navigate

That's enough now

Dropping the pen down the front of my dress and it
never reappears—I flip my skirt up in the middle of the photocopy room
while everyone hoots and hollers and I scream
WHERE IS MY PEN
someone silently hands me another but
it's not the same it never is

I think
I'm at my wit's end
which is a great relief

On the rollercoaster made entirely of wood
hissing *what were they thinking?* but you just
ignored me to focus on the feeling
whereas I didn't even feel my stomach drop
I am always
doing that

Nostalgia for a pedantry I don't possess
because that would be ridiculous and also cruel
but in the gaps I cover my mouth
pretend to cough and whisper
'would have not would of' because
you would have done
you would have.

When they issue a new ID card
proving that I do like ice cream
nobody will ever be able to challenge me again
at the party saying
'I've never seen you eat it' or
'You're lactose intolerant' or
'You only like vanilla that doesn't count'
because I will instantly end the conversation
like a struck face, so there—
which is all anyone wants:

the proper paper-cuts obtained from the proper place.
Now give me a bowl of the good stuff.

What tires us most is the delivery of it
the tone when she says
it's not what you said it's the way you said it
in such a way as to imply
well
mustn't complain
that would be mostly it would be exhausting for us and
not worth it and
take up too much time and
not enough hours in the day and
need some time to myself and
by five o' clock we're already and
besides she's probably having a rough time of it too and
we don't know her story and
what's the point and
i'm going to bed
for real this time
I won't be coming back
with family at Christmas arms
saying no I didn't mean it now you must forgive me
because I made you sad and
that hurts—
we'll call them again tomorrow
with the reference number ready for once.

I can't remember if we are supposed to be
having emotions outrageously or
only talking through the present state of things in
ways which abolish less messily
less awfully less girlishly are we done with that yet
can we talk over each other again is a poem like
can't hear you in the club
yelling through the bathroom door while you brush your teeth on the toilet
call your name on the next carriage over, yet
there is something in vogue and nobody is
tripping over themselves to tell each other what so
he turned up late to the poetry reading not—physically but

creatively. Everybody laughed I did too but I didn't know why I think he was just
counterrevolutionary or
cringey or
"cunt."

Ventriloquise an inanimate object for the
sake of the spectre and
the approval of monstrous women
who are good and
monstrous men
who are bad. It is very simple.

Every other word is only understood by five other people in the room
which is more than can be said for other universal experiences
like sex or
cooking so
it's still a relief and I clap and wave like a seal with more performative ears
like a sea lion.

On the sign was written AGICAB
but nobody took pictures for the gallery of signs
it was a private joke for public purpose
where the models don't fit
this rhythm or
structural inequity like
'she resisted; we persisted'
'she believed; he lied'
'she would rather be a rebel than a slave'
I think I'll leave it there, though
before they ask me anything else about
the sign, and the picture I took of it

It is embarrassing to write a poem
from the perspective of a brick
and we should never pretend otherwise —
not only have I never thrown one
I have never been one, so
where am I going with this exactly
except please don't fine me £100

Don't write that.

It would be easy to combine forms
poetic and governmental
which is what I am doing
because it is easy
to sign here and never know for sure,
carapace healing, when I will crack again
on the standard issue carpet or the same place
every month with the same people
who I love
who don't care about my tax returns

I don't know what's worse.

Bump, bump, bump

The policy packet crumbled in the bottom of my bag
if I open it on the bus I'll get crumbs all over my skirt
but the dog on the floor, attached to no lead,
attached to no passenger,
opens its mouth and the tongue, like wet ham, weeps.
I slip the packet back into my tote bag and pull out a
Fruit Winder
leaving my head on the window to judder and hope
that the loss of one brain cell, two brain cells, ten
will leave me room for later.
Feels like I'm renting my limbs today, in part
because of the uneven ache, in part
because there's a loan shark circling overhead, sniffing:
two stops to go, save the use of my fingers for pushing the button,
don't fidget, never that.
Write I AM EXPERIENCING HIGH LEVELS OF BURNOUT on the window
then reach for my inhaler, the bad one,
when all I want is a Classic Blue
that's what they say, I'm sure
I am an acolyte, juiced on the wedding present of my own glass hope
Thank you for coming, at such short notice
at the end of all things
on a Saturday
on your birthday
in these unprecedented times
when the traffic's bad
in the rain with his coat on
when you can barely read through the fogging lens:
It is no problem at all.

I want to gather all my friends who know and sticky keys all those I can see through the settings and never not hit that hot red dot into my arms and scream and I have not wanted to write about that because isn't it obvious but maybe it isn't if you aren't there with me ten years ago or in a few months time is running out we are slippage we feel like slippage and if it happened inside the big warehouse with the ever juddering garage doors well I want to hold them closer it is only that on special occasions they expect it and it's true but it's true on unspecial ones too that I miss you every day and then I miss you every day and I have written it now so here in the warehouse even beneath the juddering doors I am making noise where you cannot and for that I will love myself.

In summary

we do not have the necessary qualifications for
sunblock, ten tattoo needles masquerading as one
perambulating, cool across the back
a nice new pair of woollen socks and a floor
to slip over
to allow oneself the time to unslip
and not feel that like slippage in itself, so

apply to be a copywriter for blockchain
seems a scam to become
a snake tracking its own metadata
movements through the subway system
where nobody has to pay and everything is beautiful
I am my own black box this process is
dark and glittering

microchipped and sicking up the last of it
the paid-for, the direct-to, the scheduled-on
a chunk rubbed against the gullet,
lactose-lite, but on its way and I can't wait
to fry it on the pavement like it's the hottest summer
in living unmemory and I can wear my tiny shorts
completely qualified but never needing to finish.

Religious Education

I remember everything like
"Banana as proof of God" yes I do
and I'll pull it all out like a tapeworm nightmare or
menstrual needlework project or
my literal guts if I can put the rest back in like
what use is all this knowledge
three times repeated and stored forever when
I don't know what I don't know anymore and
worse, I never will

It all comes out wrong but it doesn't matter
when they do it—
or is that projection, too

When I was nineteen and learning that men like—
that men *write* the kind of poetry that requires a lot of *research*

We moved the carriage clock
but not the hands

I put his things in boxes on the front porch
like: FREE BOOKS and
wanted to tear the child's hands off when she came
not for taking what was everybody's but for
having her dad, still
one day she won't, and that's not good either
please put on some music he hated
I would rather make him mad than proud
right now

Imagine if I could even attempt an
ecopoetics

No use in that

The imagining,
I mean

When I can barely witness a man
over sixty-four without
wanting to issue a ban on men over sixty-four
it is possible I will always feel this way or
that I will feel this way for the next thirty-seven years
which isn't very KindFest 2020 of me
I can see myself now: BAN OLD MEN
but nobody thinks to ask me why
so, assumptions are made and that is bad journalism
you should have asked me so
ask me please
I can explain

The serrated edge of your own inadequacy
oh, can't even cut
can only spread

Speeding past Gnome World in excellent tears
thinking nobody has felt this much but more so me, I
have never felt this much
or maybe it's nothing, sorry

You can't look at death, I thought, then shook my head
and vomited soundly out the window,
as if I could make myself again a carsick child
to avoid the inevitable abstraction

His hands were very cold and
I kissed them.

ctrl+o

Every day will feel like a trial run
until the boulder finally catches up
so I will loudly repeat that
Leviticus is the sexiest book in the Bible
until the ground is whipped
from beneath my feet like I am a laid table
finished with, but fun.
It's a shame that the party is cancelled
because *roommates*
when Death got all dressed up for the occasion
brought their macro lens and was gonna
get all up in there:
cells, you know.
Instead I'm on the station platform like I always am in poetry
and: 'Your donations could help people like Angela.'
so: flash of 'one day i am going to live
in a nice flat with hardwood floors and a dog
and you will still be dead.'
but I'm happy for Angela, I think, and people like her.
On world leaf day we all thought about leaves
stalks leaning towards the state
so very haphazard looking,
we tried to turn them towards the sun
but they winced,
crying out for another chance to decide something,
some of their stems touched,
and who am I to bend their arc
or look out the window?
All commas are foetal now
and every time you delete one
I see it in track changes and whisper: *murderer* —
it is much easier this way.
Like a geyser of inconsistent temperature,
an occasional card with 'yay!' printed on the front,
accidentally stumbling across the blog of a
friend of a dead not-friend but distant comrade and the
tendrils of connection stiffen and crack like old foam,
I fuck up into the atmosphere

hopeful, cat on the balcony, crooning.
No I will not buy your cassette tape on the merch desk
but I will wind it for you with a ballpoint pen
because I like the sound.

Cautiously approaching absolutely fucking nothing

There's a poem about not writing a plague poem sitting on the shelf of
don't do that! it's so annoying! I have been to the base of the statue
and made my sorry mark! and then there's the great line of a pillow
on your just been sleeping cheek and a way of doing things
not dependent on a stale never have or always will
but on the fact the phone has been ringing off the hook for days
or I am in pain! or there is a stone in my shoe! or I am not held!
but don't you fucking hold me, making my tin foil chalice tin foil trophy
filling it with wine and letting it leak into my lap as though there will be
so much more in the bottle, as if we know what language will be like
tomorrow as if I can translate death back into syllabic Saxon stuff
There is no one poem I have found to feed me, baby bird and mother
in my nest of party clothes — but oh *now* we know what not to say
because everybody wants to say it, and I am thrown with great glib force
into the fact that nobody wanted me to say anything at all
which is a poem in itself, and a boring one, and I have heard it many times.

Hello World!

Without wishing to narrate or react there is only
avoidance and that is a gauche centrepiece for a caustic table
but so is this, crinoline sour clasp of hand to mouth
fingers to tongue and pull, that's good, just one more time for me
before we collect up all this obviousness from the trod ground
like complete twats and trade it back at the bar for petty cash
to do our bit and look bad doing it
but imagine, Sharpie whiskers, bodily violation, a whole train carriage,
a whole tub of marshmallows in the bath and bloating,
a whole stomach emptied into a Wendy house,
a whole life of through a scanner darkly, redly.
If there is only avoidance then it all becomes very sign my yearbook
tell me everything we never said and won't
on a coming back to town someday because we are of course
the sort of people who move away,
or that might be better still than this, to display it on a page:
this is happening, and I don't want to talk about it, but I am.
Well that's just embarrassing, and it could be any number of things.
that's the trick, confession let out of its box,
ball under cup under cup under cup
no admiration for the one who saw it move,
because they had nothing better to do—
well neither do I
but I pretend to look away, it's only polite.

Two weeks after

Well, I suppose
you could always write a bird poem

You just don't want it to have been
the first thing you did that day
that, dopamine

Coming to the realisation that it is not at all
like a river or a laketide
it is pack ice, and you are still going

There are only two ways to make a comeback:
"I am doing better" or "I no longer care"
and you are already tired of the knowing, come whenever

You have been out of sync
please hold you lightly, sticky with knowing
at the pub you will be
wanting that time you have been
storing it up you will be
releasing it like ROAR, BIG FLAME
don't laugh
or you will swallow it back down this
circus trick this
fantastic sulphur this
poison-in-waiting this,
skeuomorphing

Okay that's all.

Minor concerns addressed to the spacecraft

When you appeared I was in my pyjamas
devastated, once again
looking for an empty field to scream in
so nobody would come to my rescue,
so I could have my feelings
instead I was disturbed and I don't care if you're
very exciting, excessively limbed
I can clamber strangely too
now that you're here you have to listen

It is as if we were all on a pirate ship
with a hundred planks
walking them all just to feel like
mirage, oasis, blistering 'tell you about it later'
I would topple if I knew
there was a new board game over there
underneath
or a fresh vegetable

We all have memories of places we have never been
you can call it orientalism
or deja vu
or whining
but I remember you like a dream
before I greet you like a handshake
it's in all the movies
we both are, some of us

The usual crowd we were all
weighing up someone's worth
by whether they had a spice rack
or a spice cupboard
meanwhile there was a meteor shower
or a magician
or a firefly
like it was not his relationship to the means of production
but the exact twist of his smile
we just *knew*, the meteors just *fell*

That summer everything was made out of chiffon
as an assault to armpits everywhere
and those operating the machines
who also have armpits
I'll add it to the reading list —
sometimes it feels like a conversation starter
networking upstairs in a bookshop
just to throw over the sheets and be,
but every day I discover new implements

I check the French Republican calendar so I know what to celebrate
but you want me to toast myself
for managing it — I would rather stand in the corner
texting her,
I hate this and would rather be cooking chilli with you
and wait, there is lint in my belly button again
could you help me pick it out
I would rather not

Oh for once in my life, an arrangement of gentle fingers
a bouquet of everything
a paddling pool deep enough
a rubber tree staying as is
those high apple pie in the / sky hopes
dashed
or just magnify those ants for hours
we can do without latex, I'm sure

If you could make the album of the year into a sex toy
that would be good,
I wish the woods were bigger
but I am happy they are there at all,
but I wish they were bigger,
the summer of fuck lawns can wait
like a garden gate pun,
but it can't wait much longer

Last year when we salted some broccoli, heavily
and the smoke settled
on our knees

but I couldn't care less
about Horkheimer, right then
I only wanted to play it all again
before you had to catch the train to work
and I had to cancel therapy, but don't tell me that
drifting on determination and delusion

Like let's go to Canada let's go to Scotland
let's go disregard everyone
let's go tomorrow I am so angry you are so *right*
all the time
you're some wild garlic and I don't know
how to recognise you
but I know you're really great
because everyone says so
and nothing ever happened
because nobody ever mentions it

Want you to backdrop me
a smile against a tree,
herring gull yet to steal,
feeding hand yet to be bitten
still in the infant stages of analysis:
how do I best hold you
how do I best hold my ground
meanwhile she only went and got kettled again

It is the same in every clef:
sleep be with me
and also your breathing sounds
like a podcast, but real
I remember his house
all the clocks were set to four twenty
we are all n00bs here, I choked on it —
join my guild, I'll explain everything, just come here

When you first arrived I thought you were an omen
but now I see you're really fucking tired
I'd offer you my hand but I'm double-wielding
just reach into my pocket, take whatever's there
I don't remember but it can't be worth more
than the rolling of a wrist, held

Anyway sometimes my tongue just aches so
I request that nobody wear boots around me
for their own safety
in case of emergency
smash my face in
for justice
I will write a good piece, and forfeit 20%
to a charity of your choosing
this is, I think, the right way to be
or at least it is the right hat to wear,
the right way to wear it

I am very new here
I want to step inside
I want to feel the beam of light
I want to carry no belongings
I want to have a field day
I am obsessed
I am convinced
I am reckoning with
I am saying I am
I am suddenly realising

do you understand?

Voice I

If you zoom in you'll see I have a tiny red dot
on my forehead too,
snipers for cats, we play with phantom catnip,
soggy bags
my third eyelid closed tight but the other two
quiver and snap
it's like the carrots worked and we were right but
there's no more dark to see in
fumbling like I need more leg room or fewer legs I
cut my finger open on a penknife in july
trying to get at the butterbeans
they used glue not thread and I healed wrong
bent at the centre with nobody to blame
see, I can't really clutch like I used to
so how will they know how desperate I am —
there is only a finite amount of lead
in the polling booth pencil
and I am going to eat it all —

we are hardly a feast but when you only have
one tooth between the three of you
you learn to readjust your expectations
and your cheeks
it's like, everyone's forgotten where the mines were
and everyone's forgotten where they are right now
we dropped them like keychains and after a bit of
fishing at the grates we decided
it's only empty space, it's only hollow earth —
missing things go missing all the time
scratchcards to scratchcards, crust to crust
see, nothing is very hard to carry and I don't want to
be stuck with it
why don't we head inside with our little lasers
on foreheads of varying size and pull each other taut
until we open all over the kitchen floor and grow
moplike from the carnage.

Voice II

Darling, when the rapture comes
I want you to know that
it's okay to evangelise
it's okay to not
it's okay to want to be told it's okay
it's okay to not want to be told it's okay
everything is okay
it's okay that everything is okay,
okay? Let's begin.

Your father and I are separating —
he has taken a job as a rubber chicken
tied to the front of a removal van
and I am going to become a ball
in the breakroom ball pit
full time, this time.
When I got home I was high on pigeons
plump round droplets in lines look up forget that
hemorrhoid itch
when you were on your way to therapy
you saw: C's house, which had some
cultural appropriation in it
like weed smell,
or exposed lightbulb in the bathroom;
Marine le Pen on the basement level
window of a seaside property
built as a Victorian summer home
not to withstand the salt whip;
a Dachshund, long;
moreishness, even longer;
the feeling of being late to the organising meeting
(not very organised, is it);
and a single Camel, unsmoked but wet.

Therapy was fine but on your way home you realised
you weren't sure
if the bird bath was a war memorial or
if the war memorial was a bird bath

so you became weighed down
with a deep oysterish sadness
so addictive since you convinced yourself
if you bear down
in a squat, shell shut, you could produce something
to be worn around rich ladies' necks,
the closest you'll ever get
to literally becoming the guillotine
which would solve all your issues with alienation
as well as your deviated septum.

So you can see why we might want to leave
the digital tampon startup,
or WiFi lights flashing on the sanitary bin
you've been keeping us up all night
we never wanted a Smart Child
when we brought you into this Smart World
we never wanted you to be *connected*
we just wanted you to
learn how to cut an onion in the proper way
so we could finally
leave you unsupervised
but I have become frightened of the washing machine
since the door won't open
my clothes have taken on a new, ominous wetness
shaking fibrous fists, trapped in plastic
just you try and wear me now
they scream, and they're right —
I wouldn't dare.

Make me proud, my little welfare state,
my endless marble run,
my novelty birthday candles which last forever
but only for a little while,
and darling, stay safe out there, where things flow —
like the world is a new hire and
we're the employee equity —
we've all been burned, our tiny matchstick legs,
money-mouthed, clove-eyed, lucky.

Just leave it

He (who was very rich) told me
that to effectively burgle one had
to begin with the bottom drawer and
work one's way up,
leaving the drawers open —
less effort, less noise —
one year later
his parents' house was ransacked
but all the drawers were closed
all the silver safe.
I thought, I wish the fish knives had been taken
before he'd had a chance to teach me
what they were —
now I can identify at a distance
the most useless of things
I would rather forget.

Pippi Longstocking never watched the news

Your morning slurp, the implication of policy
skimming knots across your back
counting one two three
on the dock of the bay

another hairband lost to the ravages of
time and pockets
of it I think nothing,
only that it would be good to get out of here
for the day and leave it down
my shoulders are cold.

I always wanted dimples
and/or freckles
and/or a sunny disposition
but I am allergic to apples and
that makes it harder to spend time
outside, clambering and sitting like a tomboy heroine
pretending I could survive up there,
skinning my knees in the name of
not being a girl, and our pirate kingdom
my throat constricts just tasting
what that might have been like
if I could've stayed
longer than ten minutes without reapplying.

You spend half the time
wondering if all this is happening
because you opened a crisp packet the wrong way up
when you were ten
but the rest of the time is spent in deep meditation.

It is a privilege to make tea for you and to know how
I almost want to apologise every time
a new synapse is fired in my name
it isn't worth it, I burrow in the soil
knowing the WiFi can't reach me

down here nobody acknowledges me but the worms
and I can't tell when they do it.

Solidarity with precarious workers
solidarity with precarious rainforests
solidarity with this, the precarious grip on life itself
it is a labour and a joy to see the sun.

I take thee, in verbose analysis, to be my
trip to the shops on a cold Spring day
we are the best part of a Fab / ice / lolly:
the ensuing debate.

Remember when we all
held hands and won a Hugo award
it would be something to tell the grandchildren about
if not for everything that is.

Swilling, not yet Spring

When I stop saying 'in April' and
start saying 'in April last year',
'last April', an April less faded than this one right now
stark trickle, cubes of frozen Tixilix
must remind self
there are so many *types*
butter knife for butter not just for knife
if butter knife is knife where do all the other knives go
off rich tables
into rich drawers
working from the outside in to the very stone of me
black pudding pump
so I learned this new vocabulary
ask for the butter knife
glinting smile, cool handing
pulled like a cracker, like a limp baby.

There are women out there, thriving or something
so my grandmother had a
collection of novelty teapots
or went to bingo every week
I never got to sell her anything
like Rice Krispie cakes, or feminism,
so sit instead on the very high walls
with that very big dog
taking the jam jar shortcut to opening;
today's rubber band louder than a plane;
twisted cartoon bag of milk culture shock;
realising the album was good;
cruel candle lit: they'll call them Wellness Queens —
it's disgusting, keep pulling at our spit strings
in a flash of self-puppetry
but what else are we supposed to do
with all these lolling tongues,
say I am very sad about the way things are.

1.

I want to write about your football team
but I cannot stop crying long enough
to let you know I'm glad we didn't win
the cup.

2.

You cannot feed the ducks bread anymore
you have to feed them seed it is PC
gone mad I really want to make those ducks
explode.

3.

On days when I can only think in memes
I like to think you're turning in your urn
'rip dad you would have loved Dead Phil-
ip jokes.'

Panoptes, sweating

The bargain is as follows:
you will pretend you are Flannery O'Connor
for the summer
if you are compensated in peacocks, too

It is not necessary that the Central Intelligence Agency
should fund you
or your contemporaries
but it is preferable that they should send you a complimentary cocktail shaker
for your troubles

You and the peacocks will sit out on the porch
drinking what you are still able to drink
toasting the hue of the sky, and mourning
the lack of people to stare down
with your thousand unblinking eyes

You are a casual acquaintance and
there has been opportunity to talk and so I have been
calling you twenty-nine carat
because I don't know what it means
and there is delight beyond wealth
but not nothing for your heft and shine

So, digging through the world of my gut
to come out the other side
gasping with my head to the ground,
I have been hauling tiny sandbags to soak it up
what happens when I have for days been crackling
like cereal
with no release

On the other hand, slipping off your shoes and cavorting in the big something
learning that if I twist myself like this I wheeze
like a wrung towel
you tell me to go to Hell and I say I will bring you
back a fridge magnet

There has probably been enough said about chiaroscuro, we need
    new kinds of contrast
but I will linger one last time on the shadow of your hands making
    dog heads on the wall

In your grief you are
restoring a Furby you bought off eBay
so that it only says 'I know' —
you just really need that, sometimes

It is so sticky at night
so attached to your sheets and to everything else
you play the church and the steeple, your fingers tacky patrons

The worm at the bottom of the garden
is in league with them
these are dangerous times and
you can't afford to let him see
so you undress with the curtains
drawn for the first time

Is this a viable life
you ask yourself — and the peacocks — every morning
whether you should carry the day to term
sticking the knife in metaphor and cradling it
as it bleeds out
this is like looking in the mirror, or counting the days

I can't write either
but I do it better

You have been pretending
but the peacocks see through you
and peck you in your sleep.

Group

Go caramelise some onions go to therapy
go outside go off go
into the blue again sometime in the nineteen eighties
"Instant coffee is an Aquarius," I declare
with great confidence at the group meal
when he flips the table and leaves
because he hates the stars or anything made
with granules I cannot tell
but I say it again in that particular tone of voice
with the poems in it and he comes back
says isn't that interesting wouldn't you like to
talk about it more it is
so rare to hear a young woman
say something like that *like that*
while I replace his cutlery and calm, sharking, say
it has always seemed so obvious to me
I am a genius now and I eat my wilted greens
with great prodigious hunger.

Acknowledgments

'Minor concerns addressed to the spacecraft' was previously published on *The Hythe (The 87 Press).*

Lightning Source UK Ltd.
Milton Keynes UK
UKHW030704150322
400087UK00001B/2